First World War
and Army of Occupation
War Diary
France, Belgium and Germany

48 DIVISION
Divisional Troops
Royal Sussex Regiment
1/5 Battalion
1 September 1915 - 28 September 1917

WO95/2751/5

The Naval & Military Press Ltd
www.nmarchive.com
Published in association with The National Archives

Published by

The Naval & Military Press Ltd

Unit 10 Ridgewood Industrial Park,

Uckfield, East Sussex,

TN22 5QE England

Tel: +44 (0) 1825 749494

www.naval-military-press.com

www.nmarchive.com

This diary has been reprinted in facsimile from the original. Any imperfections are inevitably reproduced and the quality may fall short of modern type and cartographic standards.

© **Crown Copyright**
Images reproduced by permission of The National Archives, London, England, 2015.

Contents

Document type	Place/Title	Date From	Date To
Heading	WO95/2751/5		
Heading	48th Division BEF 5th Bn Roy. Sussex Regt (Pioneers) Sep 1915-Oct 1917 From 1 Div 2 Bde		
War Diary	Sailly Au Bois	01/09/1915	25/12/1915
Heading	1/5 R Sussex Regt Jan Vol. IX		
War Diary	Sailly Au Bois	01/01/1916	01/01/1916
War Diary	St Leger Les Authies	06/01/1916	31/01/1916
War Diary	St. Leger	02/02/1916	02/02/1916
War Diary	Sailly Au Bois	04/02/1916	04/05/1916
War Diary	Authie	05/05/1916	05/05/1916
War Diary	Hem	06/05/1916	31/05/1916
War Diary	Sailly Au Bois	01/06/1916	30/07/1916
Heading	War Diary 5th Battn. The Royal Sussex Regiment July 1916		
War Diary	Mailly Maillet	01/07/1916	02/07/1916
War Diary	Sailly Au Bois	03/07/1916	06/07/1916
War Diary	Bouzincourt	15/07/1916	15/07/1916
War Diary	Albert	17/07/1916	19/07/1916
War Diary	Aveluy	20/07/1916	28/07/1916
War Diary	Domqueur	29/07/1916	31/07/1916
Heading	48th Divisional Troops 1/5th Battalion Royal Sussex Regiment August 1916		
War Diary	Domqueur	01/08/1916	03/08/1916
War Diary	Aveluy	08/08/1916	28/08/1916
War Diary	Vauchelles Les Authie	29/08/1916	29/08/1916
Heading	48th Division 1/5th Royal Sussex Regt. (Pioneers) September 1916		
War Diary	Vauchelles Les Authie	01/09/1916	05/09/1916
War Diary	Longuevillette	11/09/1916	15/09/1916
War Diary	Senlis	16/09/1916	16/09/1916
War Diary	Aveluy	20/09/1916	29/09/1916
War Diary	Acheux	29/09/1916	30/09/1916
War Diary	Bayencourt	30/09/1916	30/09/1916
War Diary	Sovastre	01/10/1916	02/10/1916
War Diary	Warlincourt Lez Pas	20/10/1916	20/10/1916
War Diary	Baisieux	25/10/1916	25/10/1916
War Diary	Albert	26/10/1916	26/10/1916
War Diary	Bazentin Le Grand Wood	28/10/1916	16/01/1917
War Diary	Bailleul	17/01/1917	27/01/1917
War Diary	Cerisy Sur Somme	28/01/1917	01/02/1917
War Diary	Froissy	02/02/1917	02/02/1917
War Diary	Herbecourt	03/02/1917	20/03/1917
War Diary	Peronne	21/03/1917	30/03/1917
War Diary	Bois De Tincourt	03/04/1917	24/04/1917
War Diary	Bivouac At K.11a.54	27/04/1917	12/05/1917
War Diary	Peronne	13/05/1917	14/05/1917
War Diary	Combles	15/05/1917	15/05/1917
War Diary	Haplincourt	16/05/1917	28/06/1917
War Diary	Achiet Le Grand	03/07/1917	04/07/1917
War Diary	Hopoutre	05/07/1917	05/07/1917

War Diary	Oosthoek	06/07/1917	07/07/1917
War Diary	Poperinghe	08/07/1917	08/07/1917
War Diary	St Jan-Ter-Biezen	09/07/1917	17/07/1917
War Diary	Peselhoek	25/07/1917	26/07/1917
War Diary	Vlamertinghe	30/07/1917	03/08/1917
War Diary	Canal Bank Ypres	05/08/1917	27/08/1917
War Diary	A. 28.d.5.2	29/08/1917	25/09/1917
War Diary	W Canal Bk (N. of Ypres)	27/09/1917	28/09/1917

WO 95/27515

48TH DIVISION

BEF

5TH BN ROY. SUSSEX REGT
(PIONEERS)
SEP 1915 — ~~MAR 1919~~ Oct 1917

(FROM 1 DIV 2 BDE)

TO ITALY

WAR DIARY
or
INTELLIGENCE SUMMARY.
(Erase heading not required.)

Army Form C. 2118.

Place	Date	Hour	Summary of Events and Information	Remarks and references to Appendices
SAILLY-AU-BOIS	1/9/15		Battalion given charge of JENA & LARREY trenches – VEECHAETORIX, PARK, AUERSTAEDT, VILLARS, WAGRAM & JEAN BART in support line in addition to other work – about 12 miles of work in all to get in order & keep in order. Work continued daily on all these works – first progress made.	
"	19/9/15 21/9/15 24/9/15		Battalion provided covering to post work due SAILLY slightly shelled. 1 fatal casualty. A, B, & C Coys moved into front line trenches to gain knowledge of ground in case of an advance. No Battalion detailed to clear up, collect stores, blankets, &c. Remained there up to 27th Sept.	
"	30/9/15		Work continued to end of month	

Reg S Carglon
WCC
Comd 5th R Sussex Regt

WAR DIARY
or
INTELLIGENCE SUMMARY.

Army Form C. 2118.

(Erase heading not required.)

Place	Date	Hour	Summary of Events and Information	Remarks and references to Appendices
SAILLY-AU-BOIS	1/10/15		Ordered tracks to be constructed of RESCINGSTORIS – WAGRAM (Sunset Pit) and PAPIN – WAGRAM (Southdown Pit.) Also to take up FORT GROSVENOR & FORT DICK – under reconnaissance in front for 50 mm, in batteries for 18 mm, trench entrench near MILL at HEBUTERNE. They flew wire at FORT DICK ours is not good – but he was wire along E. side of PAPIN from the CARRIERE to NAGRAM inclusive about 350 yards of papin trench. It was a T. butt of JENA. General Institute standeen on standby for use of all units there.	
	6/10/15			
	7/10/15		Heavily shelled the lines between 12 noon & 2 p.m. with 77's, 4.2, & 5.9 guns – shots so ricochetting S.E hills sent in . . . from litter guns – 8 searchlights about 12 in attendance – no one hurt – heavy guns apparently S.E. of SERRE – the 77 & when the says now a the sers are essential	
	31/10/15		Work continued during months steadily – nearly all finished, people to using route to E. of PAPIN & revetting Furpits in FORTS DICK – GROSVENOR . Ordered trench a survey first of the CARRIERE for the III Army commenced work.	

Rod/Carpenter
WCP
C in S S.F.R. Sussex Reg.

Army Form C. 2118.

WAR DIARY
or
INTELLIGENCE SUMMARY.
(Erase heading not required.)

Instructions regarding War Diaries and Intelligence Summaries are contained in F. S. Regs., Part II. and the Staff Manual respectively. Title pages will be prepared in manuscript.

Place	Date	Hour	Summary of Events and Information	Remarks and references to Appendices
SAILLY au BOIS	6.11.15		Ordered to man FORT GROSVENOR also to platoons — as recent rains had made work very difficult, managed a relief more expeditiously.	
"	8.11.15		24 hours relief in FORT GROSVENOR — East Company R.I.R. in town for 3 days — Works continued.	
"	9 & 10/11/15		Attacks made practically in JENA & LARREY trenches owing to continuous rain - heavy rains —	
"	15 & 16/11/15		Army Review, all men employed clearing stones, mud & roads in SAILLY au BOIS.	
-	22/11/15		Draft of 4 NCOs & men from England.	
	26/11/15		SAILLY shelled with incendiary shells — About 20 fell between 4.15 & 4.45 p.m. Works continued during the whole month as far the allowance — heavy shrapnel fire occurred much — but shelters or attacks not yet completed	

Fred S. Jephson
Lt. Col.
Comdg 5 RIRE Innisks Rfs.

Army Form C. 2118.

WAR DIARY
or
INTELLIGENCE SUMMARY.
(Erase heading not required.)

Instructions regarding War Diaries and Intelligence Summaries are contained in F. S. Regs., Part II. and the Staff Manual respectively. Title pages will be prepared in manuscript.

Place	Date	Hour	Summary of Events and Information	Remarks and references to Appendices
SAILLY-AU-BOIS	5.12.15.		Village shelled about 4.6pm. The smell like a MAIZE – FORT GROSVENOR shelled intermittently – no casualties – wiring knocked –	
	7.12.15		Trench tracks to be named from JENA & LARKEY & had in hand day & programme for	
			keeping it up. Work commenced.	
	8.12.15		SAILLY shelled at 11 a.m. 2/6 p.m. No casualties	
	9.12.15		SAILLY shelled between 8.30 a.m. & 9 a.m.	
	12.12.15		Screen commenced along PAPIN on East side	
	14.12.15		New main pgun out of PAPIN Ktre remodel, as trench badly about Hf junction of felling in at sides –	
	19.12.15		Battalion Female School schoolhouse under Lieut C.R. Langham.	
	20.12.15		Orders received trench eventually 10 corrupted iron shelters in YERCINGETORIX and about 20 steel corrupted in Hot trench & downstairs Ktre. West of HEBUTERNE & FONQUEVILLERS – to be commenced. Casualties in the month very heavy digging & shore very cramped – trench of the work under fire on evacuation of sides –	
	25.12.15		SAILLY heavily shelled from 5pm to 5.30pm & from 5.55pm & 6pm about 200 shells fell – three R.G.A. killed & 3 horses – Artillery Survey first completed – No shelters & no casemates available – Shortage of timber – No bcc or spikes for casemates – Shot prepared for Tron shelters and 7 casemates Army month Army Survey first completed	

Field. Langham
Lieut.
Comm. 2 S.R.2 Sussex R.E.

48

1/5 R Sussex Regt
Jan
Vol XIII x

C.8

WAR DIARY
or
INTELLIGENCE SUMMARY
(Erase heading not required.)

Army Form C. 2118.

Place	Date	Hour	Summary of Events and Information	Remarks and references to Appendices
SAILLY AU BOIS	1/1/16		R.E. Stores taken over at 4.15 p.m. - about 60 shells - 2 hrs. bombardt - no very severely -	
ST LEGER LES AUTHIE	6/1/16		Battalion Headquarters & C & D Companies moved to ST LEGER L'AUTHIE respectively - leaving A & B Companies in SAILLY, TOUTENCOURT, Battalion H.Q., & 2 M. Guns in position - Handed over H.Q.25 at SAILLY to 2/ Lancashire Fusiliers. Major Mercer detailed to act pro tem. as O.C. SAILLY area - Military orders passed to Capt. E.A. CAZALAR & the 2/L.F.S. ROBERTS and Dr. WESTON.	
"	15/1/16		C & D Companies returned to A & B Companies at SAILLY.	
"	20/1/16		Reinforcement of 50 men received - ordered to take over charge of route to new ACHEUX - RUBEMPRÉ - MARIEUX - & sent one officer & men to be instructed in Lewis work -	
"	30/1/16		During the month 4 LEWIS guns received & the MAXIM guns called in - System adopted - Companies needed for number of fatigues also dug & rehired & parapets collected. Ordered to take H.Q.23 back to SAILLY on the 2nd prox, & to move 16Coy KAEQUERES & me to TOUTENCOURT on that day.	
"	31/1/16			

R.d.Vaughan
Lt.Col.
5th L. Cheshire Rgt.
(Pioneers)

WAR DIARY
or
INTELLIGENCE SUMMARY.
(Erase heading not required.)

Army Form C. 2118.

C.9

Place	Date	Hour	Summary of Events and Information	Remarks and references to Appendices
SOUASTRE then ST. LEGER	2.2.16		A + B Companies moved from AUTHIE to TOOTENCOURT & ARQUEVES respectively to take over work on roads in that area under C.E. VII Corps.	
SAILLY-au-BOIS	4.2.16		Battn. H.Qrs. moved here. A Coy moved from TOOTENCOURT to HEBUTERNE.	
	10.2.16		Lieut. GAMBANGER killed instantly by C.G shell while superintending work in VERCINGETORIX Trench.	
"	19.2.16		Following Coy officers now take place A W B Coy: R. SAILLY; C Coy R. SOUASTRE; D Coy R. BERTRANCOURT. O.C.D. Company Knutton is found near Louie & Lt. Townsend foot his.	
"	29.2.16		B Coy returns to permanent Sortous Shaft at FONQUEVILLERS, but & matters works. No news not Shatton were the 4 army Troops or division with 3rd Army Division with to in X Corps, 4 army. Brigade of mounts, effective strength reduced to 31 Officers + 747 other ranks – 51 R.E. to draft received – 250 men urgently needed to enable work & be proceeded with.	

Fred Caughlin
Lt Col.
Comm'g 51 Sussex
(Pioneers)

Army Form C. 2118.

WAR DIARY
or
INTELLIGENCE SUMMARY.
(Erase heading not required.)

Instructions regarding War Diaries and Intelligence Summaries are contained in F. S. Regs., Part II. and the Staff Manual respectively. Title pages will be prepared in manuscript.

C. 10

Place	Date	Hour	Summary of Events and Information	Remarks and references to Appendices
SAILLY-AU-BOIS	4.3.16		D Company report from BERTRANCOURT to BUS-EN-ARTOIS	
"	7.3.16		Major G.H. LANGHAM appointed Acting Comp. Commandant & Capts. A'127 (on probation) at TEUTENCOURT and Left. Battalion	
"	8.3.16		C Company moved from SOUASTRE to DAVENCOURT and B Coy from BONNEVILLERS to the huts HÉBUTERNE.	
"	11.3.16		A Coy relieved B Coy in the huts HÉBUTERNE	
"	12.3.16		D Coy moved from BUS to SAILLY-AU-BOIS	Pats Sgmn Msk Nosy B.M.E.
"	21.3.14		Battalion given portion of front line K2a.b.d — K sector left — handed K.9.(4,3,2,1) & K.3.(1,2) — Front line taken over by A Coy from 4th Ox. Bucks L.I. with 2 Lewis Guns and D Coy moved into Res. HÉBUTERNE. B Coy hutmented in ou. Reserve in company of training reserve b.m. & S. 1 man killed & 7 wounded.	nui Brown(1)
"	23.3.16			
"	31.3.16		Effective strength at end of month 32 officers and 942 other ranks.	

Rad Cayton
Lt. Col.
Comm 1st Rl Sussex Rgt.
(Pioneers)

WAR DIARY
or
INTELLIGENCE SUMMARY.

Army Form C. 2118.

C.11

Place	Date	Hour	Summary of Events and Information	Remarks and references to Appendices
SAILLY au Bois	1.4.16		B Coy relieve A in the left, HEBUTERNE sector, A moved to BAYENCOURT. C Coy relieved D in R. trenches R. Eff sector. D moved to SAILLY	C Coy relieved D in R
	2.4.16		A Coy moved to SAILLY	
	10.4.16		2/Lt. Strauss & 45 men of B & Army Transit instructed at VACQUERIEUX to lay reinforcements in	
	13.4.16		C Coy relieved to trenches. D Coy to K&B&A, HEBUTERNE. Came out of trenches - A Coy rest in R&B.A.	
	19.4.16		Remainder of Bn to LONGUEVILLETTE to rest & train.	
	21.4.16		22 days from train arrived.	
	29.4.16		Thirft scheme with 5 a.m. on 30% but no attack.	

Ted Roughcoin
S/Barsan (Censor)

Pioneers
1/5 R Sussex Regt
Vol 12

WAR DIARY or INTELLIGENCE SUMMARY.

Army Form C. 2118.

(Erase heading not required.)

Place	Date	Hour	Summary of Events and Information	Remarks and references to Appendices
VAILLY-au-Bois	4.5.16		A Coy in trenches at HEBUTERNE relieved by 167 Inf. Brigade.	
AUTHIE	5.5.16		Batt. H.Q. 27th with C and D Companies ordered to HEM, thence into bivouac at AUTHIE.	
HEM	6.5.16		Thence here in store whilst training with R.E.	
"	13.5.16		83 draft from England to Bnce.	
"	19.5.16		D Coy moved to VAILLY to relieve A Coy	
"	21.5.16		A Coy arrived at HEM. B Coy at SARTON relieved by C Coy & also arrived at HEM, for training with R.E.	
"	23.5.16		Attachments of 2 officers + 100 O.R., + 1 officer + 50 O.R. and of BELLE EGLISE & VAUCHELLES under Capt. C.E.	
"			Detachment of 1 officer + 35 o.r. sent to FAMECHON for fatigue.	
"	29.5.16		Ordered to return on 1st June to SAILLY au BOIS with 1st H.Q. 2 Coy to receive men of A O/S Coys to come to Division.	
"	31.5.16		O.P.s at GENEVIEVE & PAPIR with 1 offr + 18 o.r.	
			Strength at end of month 32 officers 908 o.r. Very rapid training done with R.E. during month in trenching & hostile, fortifying, rifts, loop-hole bridges etc.	

Paul Caughim
Lt Col.
Comm 5th R.C. Sussex (Pioneers)

Army Form C. 2118.

WAR DIARY
or
INTELLIGENCE SUMMARY.

(Erase heading not required.)

1/5 R Sussex Regt

C/13

Place	Date	Hour	Summary of Events and Information	Remarks and references to Appendices
SAILLY-au-BOIS	1.6.16		Batt. HQrs & A & B Coys marched here from H.E.M.	
—	2.6.16		Detachment from BELLE EGLISE rejoined.	
—	3.6.16		Draft of 35 men received.	
—	11.6.16		Draft of 58 men received.	
—	17.6.16		35 men from FAMECHON rejoined.	
—	18.6.16		Moved into Bivouac W. of SAILLY-au-BOIS	
—	22.6.16		Draft of 58 men received, & detachment from VAUCHELLES rejoined.	
—	27.6.16		Reserve shelter to "Pony" (S.H. Round firm) CSM Hart & 25 pr killed. Draft of 46 men received.	
—	30.7.16		Ordered the ready to move at 8 a.m. tomorrow in Yshire lorries to MAILLY-MAILLET to form part of Corps Reserve in ensuing operations.	
			During the month very heavy work day & night, particularly for Corps Signals. Often men working from 10 to 14 hours a day – not through the hours under fire. Night parties nearly every night – Every available man in its kilts ordered out & included Signallers, Lewis Gunners, Officers' Servants, Kitcheners & other details. Very not settled month for June & work in this month's entails and weather much difficult than usual.	

Ted Langton
W.O.
Cmds S. RE Sussex Ry.

Pioneers.
48th Div.

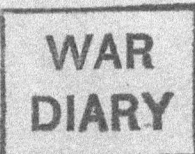

5th BATTN. THE ROYAL SUSSEX REGIMENT.

J U L Y

1 9 1 6

Army Form C. 2118.

Last entry June Diary "307/16" Ordered if necessary to carry out 1st Jan 1916 in answering operations & Mailly-Maillet to form part of Corps reserve in answering operations

WAR DIARY
or
INTELLIGENCE SUMMARY.

(Erase heading not required.)

Instructions regarding War Diaries and Intelligence Summaries are contained in F.S. Regs., Part II. and the Staff Manual respectively. Title pages will be prepared in manuscript.

Place	Date	Hour	Summary of Events and Information	Remarks and references to Appendices
MAILLY-MAILLET	1.7.16	8.30am	The Battalions & transport marched to Bertrancourt in support S.W. of MAILLY-MAILLET as part of Corps Reserve. The first time the whole Battalion & transport had been on parts together since 23/3/15.	
"	"	9.30am	Got rute march to SUCRERIE (E. of COLINCAMPS) to consolidate behind 31st Division – but there was cancelled just after the leading Company had marched away.	
"	2.7.16	7.30pm	Ordered to join & attack on German trenches between BEAUMONT and the River ANCRE which the 29th Division had failed to take yesterday. Attack to be made by 144 & 146 Brigades, each in waves on a 2 Battalion frontage. We orders to delivu as a company the attack with each attacking Battalion, so platoon to go with each Company of each Battalion. So to which front line the company were out of my hand, I decided to form a forward dump at HYDE PARK CORNER and feed in as required by Companies. The R.E. dump at ENGLEBELMER when Staff my accept in command – Capt. THOMAS. The attack was countermanded at the last moment when the leading companies were actually in the front line trench.	
SAILLY au BOIS	3.7.16	5.10pm	Arrival here in the Bertrancourt – the whole of 48th Division having moved back to their previous area.	
"	4.7.16	—	600 men entered & MAILLY-MAILLET Reservoirs new front line trench from site & MARY REDAN – M.5.E & most similar work commenced by R.C. St MORTONILE (Pionrs) from near the river ANCRE – Ref & Trench Map Sect 150 near from each Company. The new trench which to be traced was about 150 yrs to the Enemy's front line & inplaces 350 yards from our own front line. Two shafts 25 & 750 yrs from the Enemy's front line & inplaces 350 yards from our own front line. Taken over dir S'O's Park from 143 Brigade.	Ref & Trench Map Service Sheet 57 D.S.E. & N.E.
"	6.7.16		A. & D. Companies taken over Capt. CREAGHAN moved & MAILLY-MAILLET instructed to 29th Divisions & complete work – B & C Companies ordered to clear up trays as for with French trench main communication trench up & the LA SIGNY position in front of SERRE previously occupied by 31st Divisions and to establish posts & actual communication between 145 & 144 Brigades –	
BOUZINCOURT	15.7.16		Above work completed by this date – that on the new trench under particularly heavy fire causing casualties.	

1577 Wt. W10791/1773 500,000 1/15 D.D.&L A.D.S.S./Forms/C. 2118.

INTELLIGENCE SUMMARY.

(Erase heading not required.)

Place	Date	Hour	Summary of Events and Information	Remarks and references to Appendices
			nightly — Front continued vigilantly shown by officers & NCOs under very trying circumstances.	
		4.30 p.m	On this day the whole Battalion moved to BOUZINCOURT in billets as Bn Divisions were ordered to continue the attack on OVILLERS-LA BOISSELLE and POZIÈRES notably by 32nd Division. 'B' Coy + 2 Platoons of C Company moved to the Quarries by the CRUCIFIX CORNER (E.g X.7. d. AVELUY) to take over and deepen a new communication trench into the enemy front line in X.7.d. from pt 89 to pt 99 — also RIVINGTON TUNNEL to be held by a platoon as touch from the east nearest the enemy this is only 7 yards from their front trench which they still occupy at X.7.b.9.2	Ref. OVILLERS Corps 2nd 1/10000
		9.30 p.m	Remainder of Battalion withheld hold revised known intelligence positions on USNA HILL forward in rear of consolidating any gains by 143 Brigade.	
ALBERT	17.7.16	11.a.m	Received at nightly by meantime until 11.a.m. when returned with ALBERT Blcks at billets, except Nos 22 — transport then	Ref OVILLERS Sr 22 1/10,000
		2 p.m 8.30 p.m	A Coy returns trench and Communication trenches — out till 7 p.m. D Coy carried out a similar work with 105th Field Coy R.E. at LA BOISSELLE. During the night Communication trench through RIVINGTON TUNNEL into enemy front line, taken from WESTLAND TRENCH in X.1.d at X.7.b.	Refer to X/5000
"	18.7.16		Last mentioned work completed. 2 Platoons into 144 Brigade cleared up enemy front line in X.2.c. taken last night. Two Companies at ALBERT, they finally taken communication trench from X.2.a.44 to X.2.d.6.3 during the night at CRUCIFIX CORNER. Trench X.3. from 0.2 to 9.3 cleaned & deepened. 2 Lt SYMONS killed in his dug out at CRUCIFIX CORNER.	"
"	19.7.16		Trench in X.2.d. from 4.4 to 8.3. deepened to 4'6". Bullet, especially for part constructed at battle front. Trench also advanced to X.2.d.9.1. to left of 3'9" — thence to X.3.c.9.3. cleaned of this defence. Strong hostile artillery shy at DDS X.2.d.4.4. — to 8.3. — X.3.c. 0.2. — and X.8, 8.7.8	
AVELUY	20.7.16		Trench lines — Tonight's work cancelled	
"	21.7.16		Austrians dug 2ft. from X.3.d.5.2. Eppt whole strong from X.3.d.2.8 — thence Westward for total length of 800yds. Also from X.3.d.5.2. in SE direction to X.9.6.8.7. Officers with Vickers to infantry to by raid enemy barrage.	"

INTELLIGENCE SUMMARY.

(Erase heading not required.)

Instructions regarding War Diaries and Intelligence Summaries are contained in F.S. Regs., Part II. and the Staff Manual respectively. Title pages will be prepared in manuscript.

Place	Date	Hour	Summary of Events and Information	Remarks and references to Appendices
AVELUY	22.7.16		2nd Lt BLUNDER killed in working party. One company constituted carried Keep in Lat BOISSELLE. & three French Eastwards from Pt X.9.d.4.6.	Ref:OV/14/5/6 1/5000.
"	23.7.16		B"Co' worked on OVILLERS KEEP – New communication trench dug from X.3.c.9.3 to X.3.d.2.8 to depth of 3ft. Also improved first trench from X.3.c.0.7. 200 yds northwards of 100'3 V.E. (Tramway X.3.c.3.5) to a depth of 2ft. A'd platoon worked on Ruth & Tramway in ALBERT.	"
"	24.7.16		Rest of A"|C"Co worked on employed & continued on OVILLERS KEEP.	
"	25.7.16		Work on KEEP continued. Trench from X.9 & 6.6.& X.3.c.9.3. cleaned & deepened.	"
"	26.7.16		Work in OVILLERS KEEP continued – new first trench dug from X.2.d.8.7 & X.3.c.4.7. X.3.c.0.2 – 5.1 – 9.3. OK Work prevented by Gas attack.	"
"	27.7.16		Whole Battalion employed in new communication trench from X.9.c.2.0 to X.3.c.9.3. & what 3ft.	"
"	28.7.16		Battalion completed this work to average depth of 6ft. Stopping work at midnight.	
DOMQUEUR	29.7.16		Marched at 6 a.m. & took 'omnibuses from BOUZIN COURT to their for rest – about 35 miles.	
"	30.7.16		Rest	
"	31.7.16		Inspection of Equipmt, kit, arms, boots, clothing, & c.	

T.W Vaughan
Lt.Col.
Comdg V.S.R. Pioneers R.
(Pioneers)

48th Divisional Troops

1/5th BATTALION

ROYAL SUSSEX REGIMENT

AUGUST 1 9 1 6::

INTELLIGENCE SUMMARY.

(Erase heading not required.)

Summaries are contained in F. S. Regs., Part II. and the Staff Manual respectively. Title pages will be prepared in manuscript.

Place	Date	Hour	Summary of Events and Information	Remarks and references to Appendices
SENQUEUR	1.8.16		On not fit to to	
"	3.8.16		Working about R. of 4 Companies moved to bivouac at CAMP de CÉSAR (Aux L'ETOILE - SOMME) for instruction in trench warfare	
			R.E. material & material tack on 5th Augt.	
AVELUY	8.8.16		Battalion moved in buses H.1.27 to April 6 lap, Aete ridge, + C.O. to bivouac in Intermediate line near BOUZINCOURT. & Work under C.R.E. 12th Divn until letter relieved by 48th Divn. Work allotted as permanent jobs. Clean out standing OVILLERS 2nd Avenue. Line refuse of OVILLERS - Rivets & ravine 3rd & 4th N. roads from P.79. 1 - & continue dead dogs on 6 p.m. G. 1/15000. Emplacements in OVILLERS defences — MAP.	
"	9.8.16		A. Co. commenced work - Officers of other Companies reconnoitred work.	
"	12.8.16		Work at night cancelled owing to an attack.	
"	13.8.16		G.O.C. 48th Divn took over. Work continued — C+D Companies moved into bivouac in AVELUY. Early Evening	
"	14.8.16		the Subsections work handed over to Northumb. Armies & one half the Lincs & R.E. were attached preparing & improving trench right. A Coy & 4 platoon Comm: Trench between RATION & SKYLINE Trenches (X.3.a.1.5 & X.2.8.7.8.) B. Coy they not took Comm: Trench from R.33.c.9.2 to 6.9 C Coy 3 in Comm: Trench X.3.a.4.9 to R.23.c.1.4. Sister to Comm. Trench X.3.5.1.1. & X.3.a.9.5. & R.133.c.9.1. and X.26.4.9 & R.33.6.6.0.5. A. & C. were in the K. and R. SKYLINE. Trench had been reorganised by turning it a counter attack was in preparation — Also took over hammock & tramways + the Divisional. O.P. west of AVELUY, also management of tramway depot & dumps at road 74	&
"			CHIMNEY - ALBERT, on 15. Coy's front passes for 7 strong points hers from this - took continued on night 14th.	
"	15.5.16		Capt. ROSE + 2/LT Kelikman worked out new track & C.T. from dry by under very heavy fire. D. were ordered to assist in attack - had orders to make up attack unsuccessful. They according to worked further back in	
"	16.5.16		A.O.C. Companies were the to continue in support lines from Felt fire. clearing communication trenches.	
"	17.8.16		At H.G. of C. old and work, 2 Platoons of C. reached to reach work - ordered in but armour trenches -	
"	18.8.16		D. Coy went out at 2.a.m. in march to 3.C.T. to form SKYLINE & RATION Trenches & tramway, & Employing on each of 2nd & 3rd & 4th Shells with Report dump for R.E. at Pt 91. They worked upon in the first offensive, were relieved by Dr + 1/2 C. at 2.a.m. on 19th August.	&

INTELLIGENCE SUMMARY.

(Erase heading not required.)

Place	Date	Hour	Summary of Events and Information	Remarks and references to Appendices
AVELUY	20.8.16		Found 11 permanent parties of sappers at work on dug-outs at 7 different points in support line between POZIERES & POZIÈRES in front of THIEPVAL. Reconnaissance.	
"	21.8.16		Divis firm went out to find every justice for deep shelters by 144/Brigade. During operations on p.m. of A 65 & 66 2 Standing carrying parties/shelters sustained very effectively in refilling in strong counterattack. Party of sad working hands also helped by rifle fire & others in carrying of trench & heavy ammunition. At p.m.5 of 9.0 were deploying trench from X.2.a.1.6. to R.31.d.5.1. off the B.E. corner of the LEIPZIG SALIENT, then returned for parts of great strength at the morning of 22nd Aug. [Tot. of 14 sheet.]	Army. Orders. 1/50,000
"	22.8.16		2 Sections of 2 Companies (A.P.C.) sent to 143/Brigade in the line.	
"	23.8.16		The platoons working on new C.T. V.E.g K.NAB.	
"	24.8.16		2 firms relieved by firms of A & B Coys. Work on new C.T. so above continued completed.	
"	25.8.16		Permanent work continued.	
"	26.8.16		Work on dug-outs handed over to Canadians.	
"	27.8.16		3 Coy. & pl. of A. held out, they furnished out four hands forming SULPHUR AV. & RATION R. (X.3.a.31.6 x 2.6.0.) B & C Coys constructed splinter proof dug-outs in SULPHUR AVENUE. Parts at night dug out C.T. between pt. 19 in the front line in X.2.a. & started R.E. 10 a.m. on 28th Aug.	3"
"	28.8.16		Battalion marched at 2 p.m. in relief of S.W. Borderers (Divnr Batt.) 25 & div. to VAUCHELLES - LES - AUTHIE.	
VAUCHELLES LES - AUTHIE	29.8.16		In rest line - 144/Brigade still in line E. of ENGELBELMER.	

Neil Langton Lt Col.
Comm'g 3rd R.E. Sussex (Pioneers)

48th. DIVISION

1/5th. ROYAL SUSSEX REGT.
(PIONEERS)
S E P T E M B E R 1 9 1 6.

Army Form C. 2118.

1/5 R Sussex Regt

WAR DIARY
or
INTELLIGENCE SUMMARY.
(Erase heading not required.)

Vol 16

Place	Date	Hour	Summary of Events and Information	Remarks and references to Appendices
VAVEHELLES	1/9/16		At rest line — Daily training by Companies and details	
LES-AUTHIE	5/9/16		Detachments sent out to VARENNES, MONDICOURT, BEAUVAL & GÉZAINCOURT	
"	8/9/16		hunted lines	
LONGUEVILLOY	13/9/16		Reconnaissance of AMIENS defence line	
"	14/9/16		Bths continued — Moved during the night by tranches to	
"	15/9/16		hunted the same day to AVELUY.	Miss Brown (1)
SENLIS	16/9/16		Work completed —	
AVELUY	20/9/16		Sent to 11th Division — Took over work from 8th Sussex — Light railway to POZIÈRES — Tramway from AVELUY	C.16
"	22/9/16		Siding to AUTHUILLE Road — Party on AVELUY & AUTHUILLE Road dat AUTHUILLE hill — Commenced trestle bridge at BROOKER'S PASS —	
"	25/9/16		Cleaned 1st & 3rd streets & RATION trench preparatory to attack on THIEPVAL.	
"	26/9/16		THIEPVAL taken — Battalion stood by working orders.	
"	27/9/16		2 Companies (B&C) making road from POZIÈRES Cemetery N.E. towards GRANDCOURT. A & D Companies making road for guns to N.E. of the WAR valley between THIEPVAL & MOUQUET FARM.	
"	28/9/16		Same work continued.	
ACHEUX	29/9/16		Work continued on running line now reached on orders received to move — hunted at 4.30 pm to in huts in the wood —	
"	30/9/16		hunted at 10 a.m. to 6	
BAYENCOURT	"		and then came again under orders of 48th Division —	

Fred/Carson? Lt Col
Comdg 1/5/RE Sussex (Pioneers)

WAR DIARY
or
INTELLIGENCE SUMMARY.
(Erase heading not required.)

Army Form C. 2118.

C.17

48 1/5 R Sussex Rgt.

Vol 19

Place	Date	Hour	Summary of Events and Information	Remarks and references to Appendices
SOUASTRE	19.10.16		Moved here nr COIGNEUX into huts —	
"	21/10/16		A & C Coys worked on benches on right bastion at MAILLETERNE wire 1/5 M & 6 Cy R.E. — B & D Coys worked on 6th Avenue & Kellerman trenches with 3rd SMF Cy —	
			This work was continued daily and finished — Third St cleaned & repaired — Thoroughfare cleaned out — Two feet width trenches dug by N. CALVAIRE n/k MOUSETRAP sap — Mill St. cleaned out — Sumps dug in all trenches — NAB St widened — JEWISH cleaned out & repaired — huts & CAT MILL Road — Thorofare faced with huts.	
WARLINCOURT- LES- PAS	24/10/16.		Moved here to DOULLENS and thence to AMIENS.	
BAISIEUX	25/10/16		Moved here — Party of 50 men detached under 2/Lt. CAVE to work on RAILWAY near CONTALMAISON with 7 & 3rd Cy R.E.	
ALBERT	26/10/16		Moved here into Bivouacs to work under C.R.E. 1st Division. Find half bivouac cut through by our railway —	
BAZENTIN-LE- GRAND WOD	28/10/16		Work commenced. A Cy cutting work for Embanking Road E. BAZENTIN-LE-PETIT & laying same ; B Cy on road to MARTINPUICH — D Cy on main BAPAUME road from COURCELETTE to LE SARS ; C Cy on light railway from GERTAINMAISON VILLA to GUNPIT ROAD & between LE SARS & MARTIN PUICH	
"	29/10/16		Work commenced. A Cy cutting work for Embanking Road E. BAZENTIN-LE-PETIT & laying some ; B Cy on road to MARTINPUICH ; D Cy on main BAPAUME road from COURCELETTE & LE SARS ; C Cy on light railway from GERTAINMAISON VILLA to GUNPIT ROAD & between LE SARS & MARTIN PUICH	
"	3/11/16		D Company having finished BAPAUME Road brought back to work on MARTIN PUICH.	

Ken Vaughan
Lt Col.
Comm'g 5th R. Sussex (Pioneers)

WAR DIARY or INTELLIGENCE SUMMARY

Army Form C. 2118.

1/5 R Sussex Regt

Oct 18

Place	Date	Hour	Summary of Events and Information	Remarks and references to Appendices
BAZENTIN LE-GRAND WOOD	1st Nov 1916		Work continued under C.R.E. 15th Divn. as end of last month.	
	3/11/16		Commenced under C.R.E. 48th Divn. B Company to make truck track through MARTINPUICH – A Coy to make truck tracks & log track from out of tramway about M.33.c.9.6. towards EAUCOURT L'ABBAYE. Stg to do similar work from GUNPIT ROAD past DROGMONT FARM towards front line N.E. of LE SARS. Odd men, night duty men, servants etc. to construct Camp, erect AMIENS Huts, make roadway etc. Work continued by day & night as necessary until when C Company commenced on tramway S. of MARTINPUICH	
	20/11/16		B Coy commenced work on Tramway M.34.a.74 to M.28.a.25 –	
	23/11/16		Work continued to end of month –	
			During month 18 AMIENS + 10 NISSEN Huts erected + most of them completed. 1500 yards road cleared + metalled – Wash camp remetalled – Stable & Horse Standings put up – Ablution benches made – Canteen built & opened – Tool shed – Cooks stables, Stores & small sheds, Soup Kitchen, Latrines built –	

J.E.S. Campham
Lt.Col.
Comd 5 5th R.E. Sussex
(Provisional)

WAR DIARY or INTELLIGENCE SUMMARY

Army Form C. 2118.

Vol / 1/5 R Sussex Regt /19

@ 19

Place	Date	Hour	Summary of Events and Information	Remarks and references to Appendices
BAZENTIN-LE-GRAND WOOD	1/1/16		Work continued on front area on Trackboard tracks to LE SARS and to 6th Tramway. Remainder of WILLIAM, GILBERT & OBEDIENT alleys commenced. D Company employed in providing dug-out accommodation that for 1st Bn & MARTINPUICH + the platoon moved in there.	
"	15/1/16		On relief of Pioneers by 15/ Division fresh work undertaken in roads – GINZALMAISON – VILLA – MAC-NAMARA'S – BAZENTIN – MARTINPUICH + GUNPIT LANE.	
"	17/1/16		Defences of MARTINPUICH reconnoitred & preliminary plan of same prepared.	
"	21/1/16		Work commenced – also work on trackit camps at MIRACLE WOOD	
"	27/1/16		Two weeks on shelters for labour, cookers, ablution sheds to begin in SCOTS REDOUBT (N.-S.) SHELTER WOOD (N+S) ACID DROP at PIONEER Camps. Road work continued to end of month. Camps completed with material available, 23 trams huts, 12 NISSEN BOW huts, 2 Company headquarters, Stalls, latrines, food info dumps, Tank house, Lts etc. Horseshoe huts a Pub., 2 M.I. sites. Tanks: 2 M. tramways + Piving + Boilers for tap, O.D.C. finished a cookhouse K.A.6, a other H.Q.'s a Company kitchens a cookhouse finished. Bus latrines & Kitchens huts built. Transport lines under LA BOISSELLE completed. There still very crowded with huts, 5 h. Company Officers messes will in days outer. Shelter of men huts important, especially during last half of month... way to met fresh contracts +... work + care of past, etc.	

1st January 1917.

Ind. Vaughan
Major
Comdg 1/5 R.E. Sussex Rgt.
(Pioneers)

Army Form C. 2118.

WAR DIARY
or
INTELLIGENCE SUMMARY.
(Erase heading not required.)

1/5 R Sussex Regt
Vol 20

Instructions regarding War Diaries and Intelligence Summaries are contained in F. S. Regs., Part II. and the Staff Manual respectively. Title pages will be prepared in manuscript.

Place	Date	Hour	Summary of Events and Information	Remarks and references to Appendices
DEWATIN-LE-GRAND No 62	1/1/17		One month & the officially known as "CITIQUE PONT'S CAMP". all huts & numbered & marked. Works on Camp & on MARTINPUICH defences continued.	
"	15/1/17		Huts work made comfortable.	Min (Brown?)
"	16/1/17		Moved by train from ALBERT to LONGPRÉ. – Handed over camp to 15th Division. – in good condition – very slow & tedious –	
BAILLEUL	17/1/17	3 a.m.	Arrived here & rest at 3 a.m. –	
"	27/1/17		Inspected by G.O.C. 48th Div. – who praised work of Battalion during last 3 months – also congratulated bn. on report received from III Corps that the Camp at BAZENTIN-LE-GRAND & huts had been erected & framed & revisited out. – Left in an exemplary state of cleanliness & sanitation –	
CÉRISY-sur-SOMME	28/1/17		Marched here with 144th Brigade group & train – to relieve 152nd French division in front of PÉRONNE	

3rd February 1917.

Reid Cunningham
Lt. Col.
Commdg 5th (Cinque Ports Batt.)
The Royal Sussex Regt.
(Pioneers)

WAR DIARY or INTELLIGENCE SUMMARY

Army Form C. 2118.

1/5 R Sussex Regt Vol 21

Place	Date	Hour	Summary of Events and Information	Remarks and references to Appendices
CERISY s/m SOMME	1.2.17		C Company moved up by rail into trenches about 1000x N. of HERBÉCOURT. [WITTKIND Trench]	MAP 62.C
FROISSY	2.2.17		15th H.L.I. & A & B Coys marched here –	
HERBÉCOURT	3.2.17	H.1.22	marched here – R.P.C. JAMISON. A Coy to Tr. RIENZI. B Coy – ½ to H.36.C. and ½ to north of B. GUERRIERS at H.29.b. 2 Coys to FROISSY	
	4.2.17		Work consisted in maintaining Com. Tr. GUERRIERS – ROMAINS DÉFOSSÉS – & French woods, posts, shelters – Extreme cold. 30% P. labor f.f.	
	8.2.17		One section French Kdo. H.O.29. to maintain O.P.s & signal lines –	
	11.2.17		A Coy moved to FLAUCOURT – with 2 Platoons in ACHILLE in Tr. de Pénitentiaire – B. Coy retired to B Coy	
	12.2.17		2 Officers + 90 O/R – K.III W/R Rl. Coy.	
	15.2.17		B Coy moved up from FROISSY to dugouts in HÉLÈNE Tr.	
	20.2.17		Relief between C & A Coy.	
	21.2.17		A & B Coys.	
	22.2.17		During month had charge of 3 main communication trenches – numerous O.P.s, & scattered "posts", sentries between B.Gs & Bois N.d. Trenchland trucks built – track done for R.E.s & Div. details & T.M. Emplacements. 2 Div. soup kitchens erected – work as R.E. Jam sent. Very heavy work. Carried by hand. Three went trades front strong about 10 days of the month.	

Ralph Langham Col
Cmdg 1/5 R Sussex (Peiking)

/48 Army Form C. 2118.

/5 R Sussex Regt

Vol 2

C.22

WAR DIARY
or
INTELLIGENCE SUMMARY.
(Erase heading not required.)

Place	Date	Hour	Summary of Events and Information	Remarks and references to Appendices
HERBECOURT	5.3.17.–16.3.17		Interchanging relief of C & D Companies to A & B Cos	
"	17.3.17		All anticipating strength concentrated on roads HERBECOURT – BIACHES & FLAUCOURT – BIACHES eving to Evacuation to BIACHES & LA MAISONETTE by the enemy.	
"	20.3.17		1 Platoon to C & PÉRONNE Roads on billets.	
PÉRONNE	21.3.17		Bn HQ, Hd Qrs & D Coys moved to FAUBOURG de PARIS, PÉRONNE – & A Co Transport to LA CHAPELLETTE – work to continue on roads West of Somme.	
"	23.3.17		B Coy detailed for light railway from FLAUCOURT.	
"	28.3.17		D Coy moved to Biaches to S.W. corner of Bois de BAIZE & A Coy to TANCOURT Station forward roads – B Coy to PÉRONNE tracks on roads radiating from there –	
"	30.3.17		C Coy moved to ROSSU to take over intermediate roads, the roads allotted to A Co being extended eastwards as the enemy is driven back.	

2.4.17.

Neil Carpenter Lt Col.
Comm'g 5th R Sussex Regt
(Pioneers)

Army Form C 2118.

WAR DIARY
or
INTELLIGENCE SUMMARY.
(Erase heading not required.)

1/5 R Sussex Regt
Vol 23

Place	Date	Hour	Summary of Events and Information	Remarks and references to Appendices
Posts at TINCOURT	3.4.17		Had parties wiring from b Bivouac - about T.12.b.33 - C Coy to MAP. 62.C.NE 1/20000
"	2.4.17		Quarry K.5.c.9.2. B Coy to ST.EMILIE. B Coy to Bivouac in GRUBS WOOD - E.27 Central.
"	3rd 4.17		A Coy (Rees & Rickson huts) road to ST.EMILIE. (E.18.C.75)
Bivouac at R.11.a.54	27.4.17		Had parties working here in trenches -
			Work during month - all roads in forward area; erection of Adrian huts, building Hrs Quarters for 48th Divn; filling numerous craters, laying stone fronts & communication trenches, wiring & consolidating positions formed at TIMBER'S, SAIGE & 62 C NW Chaulkke dipt.
			PETIT PREEL & GUILLEMONT FARMS -

3/4/17

Fred Campion
Lieut Col.
Comm'g 5th R.E. Sussex Regt.
(Pioneers)

C. 23

Army Form C. 2118.

WAR DIARY
or
INTELLIGENCE SUMMARY.
(Erase heading not required.)

15th R. Sussex Regt.
Vol 24
C-24

Place	Date	Hour	Summary of Events and Information	Remarks and references to Appendices
BAPAUME 6th M.C.a. 54	3.5.17	noon	42nd Division relieved by 42nd Division. We stay in the line for the present?	
"	7.5.17		Scouts (acting as Artillery O.P. Observers) withdrawn after 3 weeks constant observation work for Division.	
"	8.5.17		Scouts to FLAMICOURT for rest & training.	
"	11.5.17		All work ceased and most of night spotting parties – officers 15 hrs reconnoitring fresh work. D.Coy to PÉRONNE.	
"	12.5.17		Remainder of Battalion marched out to PÉRONNE.	
PÉRONNE	13.5.17		1 Platoon each of B & D moved to HAPLINCOURT to relieve Bn.H.Q. near BEAULENCOURT.	
"	14.5.17		Scouts moved to BEAULENCOURT to take over Div'l O.P.s to be run from 40th Div.	
COMBLES	15.5.17		Marched here via Albu.	
HAPLINCOURT	16.5.17		Marched here via CAILLY-SAILLISEL. Reconnoitring our sector.	
"	17.5.17		B & D Coys moved up into Brigade res. VÉLU.	
"	19.5.17		A Coy moved up to Brigade West of VÉLU. "B" & "D" to HERMIES – BEAUMETZ – DOIGNIES line - "A" to BEAUMETZ-MORCHIES line –	
"	20.5.17		C Coy training & resting at HAPLINCOURT.	
"	26.5.17		15th Coys moved up to position regarding line – BEAUMETZ – MORCHIES – no far hints on the CAMBRAI road.	
"	31.5.17		A & C Coys relieved B & D Coys. Stay returned to rest. B Coy took over west of A Coy. During month big few reinforcements. Lost 2 Officers & 67 O.R. wounded from III Corps Light Railway Coys. At end of month Effective strength 39 Officers & 840 O.R.	

Paul Verplanh Lt. Col.
Comdg 15 R Sussex Regt. (Pioneers)

WAR DIARY
or
INTELLIGENCE SUMMARY.
(Erase heading not required.)

Army Form C. 2118.

1/5 R Sussex Regt

Vol 25

mi Chapman C.25

Place	Date	Hour	Summary of Events and Information	Remarks and references to Appendices
HAPLINCOURT	7/6/17		No 1 Platoon on farm from No 3 (A Coy?) under 2/Lt TRAVERS employed to consolidate an emergency post taken by the Bde Patrol. Work hopes not towards after two hrs & renewed within 10 minutes & being completed by dawn without a casualty.	HERMIES H.26.a.9555
"	8/6/17		Same party completed work on front left centre line of infantry - Corps wire gap, & improvement generally. satisfaction with work.	
"	12/6/17		Relief of A & D Companies – B Company to neighbourhood of HERMIES.	
"	13/6/17		A Company to road S. of MORCHIES	
"	14/6/17		B Company to sunken road S.E of BEAUMETZ & C Company into Hut Camp — all Italian named Rest ready Knowe North of fire XIII Corps nr POPERINGHE.	
"	28/6/17		Work during month 1/6/17 by 1/5 HERMIES — DOIGNIES line & construction of dug outs – Strength at end of month 41 Officers & 1085 O.R.	

1st July 1917

Neil Vaughan Upr.

Cmnd 1/5 R. Sussex Regt (Princess)

WAR DIARY or INTELLIGENCE SUMMARY

Army Form C. 2118.

/5 R Sussex Rgt
Vol 26

Bois Brun (?)

Place	Date	Hour	Summary of Events and Information	Remarks and references to Appendices
ACHIET-LE-GRAND	3/7/17		Bn relieved by 2/2 KRRC (moves 31st Div) & marched here. CO went forward to XIII Corps near N.g YPRES.	
	4/7/17		Brigade Training May manoeuvres. Inspected by G.O.C. 38/DIV. who informed his satisfaction with work done & my retire during travel in to Bn HQ. & H.Q.	
HOPOUTRE OOSTHUEK	5/7/17		Moved here by train & marched into bivouac at improv A.24.b.c.d.	Beselare Sheet 28 1/40000
	6/7/17		Bivouac strengthened, baths, party bathed.	
POPERINGHE	8/7/17		Moved off 1.30.p.m. ... killed ...	
SOMMERUILS-BUZE	9/7/17		Moved here & cont. 2.	
"	10/7/17		Reconnaissance of forward works 6 Co officers Contractors.	
"	11/7/17		B. Coy detailed for light rail construction.	St. Julien. 28. N.W. 2
"	12/7/17		Met A. & B. Coy. & Company No 3 ... hire gang of 6. Sorry - 6. B. Coy	
	13/7/17		C + D Coys moved to CANAL BANK at I.1.8.75. Transport to PESELHOEK	
	16/7/17		Handed over to 13th Battn & moved to Bivouac at A.15.a.73. (PESELHOEK)	
	17/7/17		C + D Companies moved back - the huts ... general use on CANAL BANK.	
	26/7/17		A Coy. went to Bivouac at H.A.c.90 (N.E. of VLAMERTINGHE)	
PESELHOEK	27/7/17		HQ 2 + C. D. Coys moved up - Bivouac with A Coy. - in anticipation battery "July". (No 2 Platoon formed in rifle)	
VLAMERTINGHE	29/7/17		YPRES. 2 Platoons of D. Coy moved out at 2.45.a.m. & open bloody rush ...	
"	31/7/17		Commencement of 3rd Battle of YPRES - Remainder moved up #7.a.m. & gunner of BUFFS bomb by 9.45. a.m. N.g. HAMMOND'S OPENED ATTACK to engage - Being rested on maintenance from 4 to 9 pm. Go pr to the to # hit set tripl ... Called prone, then things ... transport ... Abt 100 men ... killed & 8 officers ... during the month, inc. 6 on my platoon.	C. 26

Reid Carghan
Lt. Col
Comdr. 15th R Sussex Regt
3/8/17

WAR DIARY
or
INTELLIGENCE SUMMARY.

Army Form C. 2118.

5 R Sussex P/48

Vol 27

C.27

Place	Date	Hour	Summary of Events and Information	Remarks and references to Appendices
YLAMERTINGHE	1/8/17		Continued work on TYPES 9 & 10 & other about ADMIRALS Rd in prep for the battle pending here WINIZE	
	3/8/17		Refine arrangements & rehearsal	
CANAL BANK	5/8/17		Moved into West CANAL BANK (about C.25 d.) ready for our present work.	
YPRES	6/8/17		Began Sunday night work in BUFFS Rd Farm ADMIRALS Rd up in CALEDONIA SUPPLY (C.22.b.1090)	
	16/8/17		Regular attack on Enemy line EYR STEENBEEK. Two platoons under Capt CREAGHAN taking F ALBERTA	
			Forestalled my proposed period. Arty on platoons of D Coy were attacked to Tank Null which was in their	
			Sug'tc. Casualties 6W-CREAGHAN killed, P.W. GREEN having been killed. The remainder of the 2 platoon formed	
			up BUFFS Rd / YR KITCHEN Rd as far as VAN HEVLE FARM.	
	18/8/17		Commenced york at first ascent down over HILLTOP & ENGLISH FARMS.	
	19/8/17		2 Platoons yC formed A HILLTOP FM	
	20/8/17		(consisting of C under O. HILLTOP FM	
	21/8/17		2 formed to new ENGLISH FM	
	22/8/17		A Coy unloaded TRAMWAY in the vicinity of TEW HILL	
	23/8/17		Relieved by 10 R.I. Rifles (Anhurst (rue 56.5.35b) & unmoved this with H+2 m - C.5.26.g. A.Coy moved to SEGARD FERME	
			H.4.c.49 (East of RUMMERTINGAS)	
	29/8/17		A.Coy commenced work on B+ S Rd East y ASYLUM 28.	
			Every Co took 073 Company continued work on 218ht Railways detachment.	
A28 & 5.2.39/8/17			A casualties Rail jj officer killed, one slightly wounded during formuning - Casualties are	
			immense but most of the last wounded returning Responsive fully on lead in eff either	
			working strength getting two Cars - 2 Platoons being possibly employed.	

Reuby Coughan Lt Col
Cmr 5 R Sussex

1/5 R Sussex Vol 28

C.25

Army Form C. 2118.

WAR DIARY
or
INTELLIGENCE SUMMARY.
(Erase heading not required.)

Instructions regarding War Diaries and Intelligence Summaries are contained in F.S. Regs., Part II and the Staff Manual respectively. Title pages will be prepared in manuscript.

Place	Date	Hour	Summary of Events and Information	Remarks and references to Appendices
A.28.d.5.2.	8/9/17		Since beginning of month, "A" Coy's have continued work on Forward Roads –	BELGIUM & FRANCE 22. N.W.
"	9/9/17		A. Coy came back here from B. C&D Coys moved to camp at H.4. a.4.9 & had additional accommodation –	
"	10/9/17		C Coy commenced work on BUFFS & ADMIRALS road – B Coy on the Battle in O.G. train 1&2.	
"	12/9/17		B. Coy rejoined from Light Railway work.	
"	23/9/17		C & D Coys moved to rest camp at B.29. 8.64.	
"	25/9/17		A Coy relieved C Coy in employment of front reduction of Cutter by cementation –	
W.CANAL B.K	27/9/17		H.Q. 2 Coy with A.B & D Coys moved here – & C. to Bristol Farm (H.10.a.57) Transport & MARSHES in H.3.B.	Nil Brig (2)
(N. of YPRES)				B.G. 28, N.W. 2.
"	28/9/17		A Coy commenced work on ST JULIEN – WINNIPEG Rd. – B. Coy on ST JULIEN – TRIANGLE F.M. road – B.G. & D. Coy R.E. on Trenchboard Tracks under O.C. 475 F. Coy R.E.	

Very few reinforcements received during the month. – Casualties heavy – Companies in temporary rest trained in drill & musketry –

3rd Oct. 1917.

Fred Stephens
Major
Comm'dg 1/5 R.S. Sussex Reg
(Pioneers)

www.ingramcontent.com/pod-product-compliance
Lightning Source LLC
Chambersburg PA
CBHW081248170426
43191CB00037B/2087